Cleaning Up the Quill Lakes' Catastrophe
(Ayden's Adventure™)

Rosanna Gartley

A Mouse Gate™ Adventure

Mouse Gate Press
1103 Middlecreek
Friendswood, Texas 77546
281-992-3131 TEL
www.MouseGate.com

All rights reserved. Except as permitted under the United States Copyright Act of 1976, no part of this publication may be reproduced, stored in a retrieval system, or transmitted in any form or by any means, electronic or mechanical, or by photocopying, recording, or otherwise without prior permission of the publisher. Exclusive worldwide content publication / distribution by TotalRecall Publications, Inc.

Copyright © 2018 by: Rosanna Gartley
All rights reserved
Edited by: Rosanna Gartley
I ISBN: 978-1-59095-354-9
UPC: 6-43977-43541-5
Library of Congress Control Number: 2018934162

Printed in the United States of America with simultaneous printings in Australia, Canada, and the United Kingdom.

FIRST EDITION
1 2 3 4 5 6 7 8 9 10

Cover photo by John and Rosanna Gartley.
Fleuron downloaded from fotolia were created by chee siong the.
This is a work of fiction. The characters, names, events, views, and subject matter of this book are either a product of the author's imagination or are used fictitiously. Any similarity or resemblance to any real people, real situations, or actual events is purely coincidental and not intended to portray any person, place, or event in a false, disparaging, or negative light

The scanning, uploading and distribution of this book via the Internet or via any other means without the permission of the publisher is illegal and punishable by law. Please purchase only authorized electronic editions, and do not participate in or encourage electronic piracy of copyrighted materials. Your support of the author's rights is appreciated.

Dedicated to my grandson, Ayden, whose imagination and ingenuity will enable him to accomplish anything! Dedicated also, to those who love, support and encourage him.

—Grandma Rosie

Acknowledgments

Thanks to my husband, John for all his support, my sister, Mariette for her input, Todd and Ducks Unlimited Canada and to my publisher, TotalRecall Publications, Inc.

A special thank you to Tom, the Wynyard Co-op and the Wynyard Advance for your help with the cover.

The Book

Eleven-year-old Ayden has lived on a farm near the Quill Lakes all his life. When the lakes' flooding puts his family at risk of losing their livelihood and way of life, something must be done. Ayden connects with some uniquely talented forest creatures, uses an ample dose of Disney Magic and relies on his own ingenuity to solve his community's water-logged problem.

The perfect Storytime book for both boys and girls ages 8–12 Grades: 3–6.

Chapter 1

Eleven-year-old Ayden squirmed in his desk seat, unable to focus on Mrs. Y. Chorney's lesson. He swiveled his head around to look at the clock hanging on the classroom's back wall, only to be disappointed. The hands had only moved three dots since he had looked last. With a sigh, Ayden turned to face the front again, slumping impatiently in his seat when he caught sight of his twin sister, Mya, paying attention, as usual. He knew she would be anxious for dismissal, too, because today was dance class for her and their younger sister, Alyxa. Ayden would not be tagging along, he was going combining! He had already finished his math page and turned his attention to what he could see out of the classroom window. The cobalt blue sky was cloudless and the sun's rays warmed Ayden's back. He could see a few parents' vehicles parked at the curb waiting for Wynyard Elementary School's dismissal bell to ring. At exactly 3:20 the bell buzzed and the once quiet classroom came to life. Papers rustled, children chatted and above the noise Mrs. Chorney raised her voice to remind the students of an upcoming quiz. Ayden grabbed his backpack, yelled a good-bye to his favorite teacher then sprinted toward the school bus. Despite being first to his seat, he knew the bus would not be moving until all of the students climbed aboard. He hoped everyone was as anxious to get home as he was.

After what seemed like the slowest ride home EVER, the bus stopped in front of Melsted Farms. Ayden raced both of his sisters off the bus and ran all the way to the house. He kicked off his shoes and dropped his backpack, then quickly changed from his school clothes into an old tee shirt, jeans and brown coveralls. His running shoes laid on the rug because this job called for work boots. He no longer needed help lacing them up and when he finished, he plucked his John Deere cap off its door knob perch and bolted out the back door with his Mom in hot pursuit.

"Ayden get back here," she said sternly.

Ayden stopped in his tracks and rolled his eyes. He didn't think he would be lucky enough to make a clean getaway. Turning around to face her he replied, "What Mom?"

"How about you take a snack with you?"

"Oh, okay," he replied, reluctantly walking back into the house. He grabbed an apple from the brown, pottery, fruit bowl that sat on the kitchen island and took the two cheese sticks his Mom held out for him. He made no secret of the fact that his Mom's interruption was annoying, yet he admitted to himself that he was lucky to have a mom who took such good care of him. With his snacks stuffed into his side pocket, he ran down the four steps and jumped on his mini-quad. With a turn of the key, the engine purred and Ayden was off to where the trucks were emptying their huge loads of grain.

Ayden's Papa John was standing beside the large truck watching the auger suck up the grain and spit it into the small, round opening on top of the storage bin. The young boy parked his quad close to a shed, well out of the way of the trucks and machinery. In busy harvest time, safety awareness was especially important and Ayden had heard the speech many times. Papa John gave his grandson a smile and a friendly wave, motioning for him to climb into the truck's cab. Ayden hoisted himself onto the well-worn seat. The truck stunk like dirt, grease, dust and grain, many of his favorite smells. It was hot in the cab and Ayden cranked down the window hoping to feel a breeze. The loud motor of the auger stopped as Papa John closed the opening at the end of the truck box and climbed into the cab. Once inside, he pushed a lever and the truck box levelled out so they could head back out to the field for another load of wheat.

"Hey buddy, how are you today?"

"Good," smiled Ayden.

"How was school?"

"Okay."

"Ready to get to work?"

"You bet!" said Ayden, while he offered his grandpa a cheese stick, knowing it was one of his favorite snacks.

"Thanks," said his Grandpa peeling away the wrapper as he encouraged the old truck to move forward.

Ayden was all smiles as he settled back into the grimy seat enjoying the sights and smells of late summer. He knew the combine was somewhere up ahead and he couldn't wait to see it. Sure enough, within a minute, he could see a cloud of dust in the field, west of the road. That dust was coming from their combine. Papa John carefully drove the truck off the road onto an approach then down into the section of the field that had already been combined. The leftover wheat straw standing like stiff wire, scraped the bottom of the truck's axels as the giant truck rumbled through the field. It took no time for the truck to catch up to the slowly, creeping combine. As soon as Ayden's Dad spotted his son in the truck, he stopped the large machine so Ayden could climb aboard.

It would have been difficult to wipe the grin from the young boy's face. This is what he had been thinking about all day while he was supposed to be paying attention to his teacher. As Ayden closed the door behind him, his Dad started the combine on its slow crawl, allowing the complicated contraption to separate the wheat kernels from the chaff.

"Hey bud, how are you doing today," asked his Dad, not taking his eyes from the crop in front of him.

"Good now," smiled Ayden, "How is it running?" he asked, meaning how thick was the grain being harvested.

"It's a good crop, heavy and dry, ideal conditions for combining. Did Mom take the girls to dance class?"

"I don't know, I guess so. I left before they did."

"Remember, you have school tomorrow, so you can't stay out here too late."

"I know Dad, but I don't have any homework and having a shower before bed doesn't take very long," reasoned Ayden.

"When your Mom texts and says it's time for you to head home, I don't want to hear any arguing."

"I know Dad," replied Ayden, as he watched a field mouse running for its life ahead of the combine's cutter bar. Soon the hopper was full of wheat kernels and Papa John had pulled the grain truck beside the combine's auger allowing it to unload its treasure. With the combine in park, Ayden and his Dad stepped out of the cab to stretch their legs. Looking out over the landscape,

Ayden's Dad placed his hands on his hips and shook his head from side to side while letting out a long, loud sigh. Ayden stood on his tippy toes to try to figure out what his Dad was looking at but all he could see were acres and acres of wheat and canola.

"What are you looking at Dad?"

"Just how much water there is out there."

"But Big, Middle and Little Quill Lakes have always been there, right?"

"Yes, but the lakes overflowed their banks more than ten years ago and have become huge, flooding a lot of our farmland. Land we can't make a living from anymore. What is covered by water won't be good for anything in the future."

"Because it would be too wet?"

"Well, that and because the water is very salty. Even if the soil dries out, the salt will stay and our crops won't grow in salty soil. The worst part is that each year the flooded lakes grows bigger." Ayden could see the concern written all over his Dad's face. He had heard talk around town and noticed some articles in the local newspaper about the flooding but he had not realized it was affecting his own family, until now.

"Remember Grandpa Bruce's bronze plaque that was in the marsh Ducks Unlimited named for him?"

"Yes." Ayden remembered sometimes on the way to Saskatoon, their family would pull over on the highway and walk to the edge of the marsh. It was named Melsted Marsh and there had been a very large wooden sign and a plaque on a post explaining who his Grandpa Bruce was, and why the marsh had been named for him.

"The sign and the plaque had to be removed because of the flooding."

"Oh no."

"Both would have been ruined if they had been left where they were. Ducks Unlimited has them in storage for now, so they are safe. Maybe someday they can be put up again."

"How can the flooding be fixed?"

"That's a great question, bud. Many engineers and water specialists have been here trying to figure out how to help. Trenches could be dug so the extra water could run into other lakes in the area but once again, salt is the problem. The lakes and rivers around here are all fresh water and no one wants to see them contaminated with the Quill Lakes' salt. But something better be done soon, we have lost hundreds of acres of farmland and some people have lost their whole farms, including their homes. Ayden couldn't imagine their house being swallowed up by water. He looked past the fields and he could see a thin slice of blue water shimmering all the way to the horizon. What once looked like a huge swimming pool to Ayden, now looked like an enemy.

It was nearly dusk when Ayden jumped up into

Papa John's grain truck for the ride back to his quad. He had had a great evening with his Dad and Grandfather. He had even been allowed to steer the combine for a short while, just like a real farmer. Now that the sun was going down, he could smell the moisture of the dew settling on the ground. Without a breeze to keep the grain dry, combining for tonight would come to an end soon after the sunset. Ayden maneuvered his quad home, parking it near the garage, then made his way into the house.

Judging by the giggling and splashing he could hear, he knew his sisters were probably getting ready for bed. After removing his dusty work boots and overalls, he washed his hands in the bathroom sink. A quick glance in the mirror told him he wouldn't escape without a shower. His blonde, curly hair was covered in dirt and dust with the only, somewhat clean part of his face hidden behind the lenses of his glasses. But getting clean would have to wait, he was starving. Ayden opened the fridge to see what his Mom had made for supper. Spaghetti and meat sauce sat right on the middle shelf making him smile. It was his favorite food. He heaped a plate full of the pasta and sauce and placed it in the microwave. While waiting, he munched on a few grapes that hung out over the edge of the fruit bowl. The microwave dinged, signaling his meal was ready. Oh no! He was in trouble now! He had forgot to cover his food and now the microwave was covered in red splatters. He carefully lifted the hot plate out and sat it on the counter while he poured himself a large glass of milk.

The girls, dressed in their pajamas came giggling out of Mom's bedroom for a bedtime snack.

"When did you get home?" asked Mya.

"A few minutes ago. I got to drive the combine," boasted Ayden.

"You did not!" replied Mya.

"Did too. Just ask Dad," he said, slightly raising his voice, "I got to drive it one whole length of the field." He hoped the added details would make it more believable. Mya finished peeling her orange feeling a little jealous.

"Well Mom, Alyxa and I played a couple holes of golf after dance class," replied Mya, hoping to make Ayden a little jealous too.

"Big deal, I can do that anytime."

"Hey buddy," said Mom, "I didn't hear you come in. Good, you found something to eat. Finish your supper then it's into the shower, then bed. No time for LEGO tonight."

"I know." Other than hockey and farming, Ayden's other passion was LEGO. He had been building with it since he was two years old. He and his Dad had assembled many intricate models that he proudly displayed on shelves that took up a whole wall in his bedroom. With thousands of

LEGO blocks organized in drawers, he had an almost endless supply. With imagination and skill, he made good use of the blocks. To Ayden, it was much more than a hobby.

After a quick shower, Ayden set his glasses on his desk then climbed up onto his bunk bed. His Mom leaned up and kissed him good night while she ran her hand through his damp, blonde curls. He could hear his sisters in the next room climbing into their beds. He was glad he didn't have to share his room; he liked his things to be organized and untouched. Laying quietly, tucked under the blankets, his thoughts slid back to the field and the combine he had driven. Then, as he drifted off to sleep, he remembered the flooding of the Quill Lakes.

Chapter 2

The tiring harvest season was drawing to a close. Life on any farm was always turned a little inside out and backward during the busy times of year. Farmers had no choice but to spend many hours in the field, working to get the crop in the bins before Mother Nature passed over the fields with her frosty wand. The only time the kids had seen their Dad, lately, was when they visited him on the combine. Every day, he was gone before they got up and wasn't home before they were asleep. Harvest time was also hard on their Mom. She had to take care of everything on her own from breaking up sibling quarrels, grocery shopping, cooking all the meals and taxiing the kids to and from their activities. Everyone in the Melsted house was smiling more these days as the end of harvest neared.

Ayden's Dad farmed with his older brother, Ryan. Both families' kids were best friends and only lived down the road from each other. When harvest officially ended, the two families gathered for a wiener roast celebration.

"Hi Aunty Kayla," Mya said, grinning from ear to ear as she entered her aunt's kitchen.

"Hi, sweetie, what do you have there?" pointing to the container Mya carried.

"I baked some cookies and Alyxa helped me decorate them," Mya answered proudly. "Hi Cooper," said Mya, to her eight-year-old cousin as he ran into the room.

"Hey Mya, wanna go outside and help my Dad start the fire?"

"No thanks, but Ayden is already out there. Where is Dylan?"

"Up in her room." Mya placed her cookies on the kitchen counter and raced up the stairs to her cousin's bedroom.

"Hey, Dylan, you ready to go outside?"

"Yep! Just putting my hair up in a pony." The two girls headed down the stairs then passed through the kitchen where both of their moms were gathering hot dogs, buns and all the fixings.

"Wait a minute, you two. Each of you grab something to take out to the fire pit," called out Mya's Mom. With their hands full, the girls headed outside to join the rest of their families.

❖❖❖❖❖ ❖❖❖❖❖ ❖❖❖❖❖

The hot dogs were black and crunchy, the bun soft and the mustard tangy; just the way Ayden hoped they would be. He had to eat three of them before he started to feel full then topped off his meal with some veggies and dip followed by several slices of juicy watermelon and two of his sisters' cookies. Darkness overtook the yard, forcing everyone to put on jackets despite the warmth of the fire's dancing flames. Uncle Ryan placed a few more logs on the fire, causing bright orange sparks to fly into the night sky. The flames were mesmerizing, but to Ayden, the best part of any campfire was the smell. The smoky, woodsy smell always made Ayden feel happy. He closed his eyes listening, smelling and sensing everything around him. He could feel the warmth of the fire on his face and chest, while the cool, damp air chilled his back. He could hear the crackling of the logs, the conversations of the grown-ups and the laughter of the three girls who were goofing off several meters away. He knew Cooper was sitting next to Aunty Kayla while five-year-old Oliver, was already asleep with his head against Uncle Ryan's shoulder. Ayden felt like he could sit here forever, content, with his family around him. Suddenly his Dad stood up.

"Hey everyone," he spoke, breaking into Ayden's thoughts. "Come here, girls." The girls quit their giggling and came closer to the fire. Oliver stirred while everyone else perked up wondering what he was going to say. "Harvest is over and the farm had a good year. What would you kids think about all of us going on a vacation together?" There were shouts and yesses from all over the place.

"Where would we go?" asked Cooper.

"How about Disney World?" That brought about squeals and screams, laughter and a whimper as Oliver was startled awake.

◆◆◆◆◆ ◆◆◆◆◆ ◆◆◆◆◆

The plane landed in Orlando with all ten family members on board. The four adults remained composed while the luggage was collected, while the children's behavior mirrored their excitement. The boys sat on nearby chairs, laughing at some inside joke, Alyxa giggled nonstop beside her Mom while Mya proceeded to let off pent up energy by doing cartwheels next to the luggage carousel. With suitcases in tow, the group headed outside to wait for the hotel shuttle. It felt good to be outside without a coat and to feel the warm, Florida breeze.

The two families settled into their hotel suites, unpacked and ordered pizza for supper. Bedtime tonight would be early, for tomorrow promised to be a day packed with excitement. Both families had enjoyed Disney World several times before, knew the lay of the land and agreed to spend the first day together in the park.

The next day, all six kids were up annoyingly early. After a quick breakfast, the families were shuttled to the main gate of the Magic Kingdom. Everyone rode multiple rides, ate some sticky, sweet food, walked for miles and saw some amazing sights. At the end of the day, exhaustion took over and both kids and adults tumbled into bed, looking forward to the rest of their vacation.

On day two, togetherness gave way to differing interests. The younger boys stayed at the Magic Kingdom with Uncle Ryan while the girls and Ayden went to Downtown Disney. The three girls had appointments at the Bibbity Boppity Boutique so Aunty Alana and Aunty Kayla accompanied them, while Ayden and his Dad made their way to one of Ayden's favorite places, the LEGO Imagination Center. He had been there several times before and each time he was more impressed than ever. There was always something new to see and lots to buy. The hard part was narrowing his choices down to what he couldn't live without. He knew he couldn't buy everything.

Ayden took a step inside the store and paused. His Dad stood behind him smiling. He knew his son was pleasantly overwhelmed with a whole store full of his favorite toy.

"What do you want to look at first?" asked his Dad.

"I don't know. I think we should just start on one side and go all the way around," suggested Ayden, pointing to his right.

"Okay, bud, lead the way."

"Wow! Look Dad, look in here," said Ayden as he ran up to a large plexiglass cube holding an impressive structure. "I might want this."

"We'll see."

"No wait! Maybe this one."

"How about we look at everything before you try to make a decision." In silent agreement, Ayden moved on to look at the kits that lined the store shelves. Time was going by quickly and it wouldn't be long before the girls would be meeting them there. "Probably about time to make some decisions, Ayden. Have you figured out what you want?"

"Yep! I know!" Ayden and his Dad carried the special boxes to the counter. He was able to spend last year's saved Christmas and birthday money on a few kits, while his Dad had agreed to buy one for him as well. Just as they were paying, the girls entered the store. All three had worn their princess dresses. They had had their hair done, make-up applied and nails painted. Ayden looked at them and rolled his eyes. He just didn't understand. *What a waste of money,* he thought to himself, *one shower and the hair and make-up would be gone.* But all he said out loud was "girls!" while he rolled his eyes, once again.

Before climbing back into the van for the ride back to the hotel, they all walked towards the lake to see the huge, permanent LEGO structures that stood next to the LEGO store. The giant dinosaur was always a favorite but today, Ayden gravitated toward the gigantic bulldozer made entirely out of blocks. A real engineer had designed it and it had taken many people weeks to build. The giant structure garden was one of the few places Ayden would happily agree to have his picture taken; and he hated having his picture taken.

"Ayden, put on that hardhat and pose by the bulldozer for a picture." Ayden walked to the front of the giant machine and placed the yellow hardhat on his head... His Dad took a moment to position the camera then pressed the button... and that's when the magic happened!

Chapter 3

It was as if the sun shone directly into Ayden's face when his Dad snapped the picture. A blinding, white, light forced him to close his eyes and when he opened them he was no longer in Downtown Disney but back in Saskatchewan. His heart skipped a beat and he anxiously looked around. *Wait a minute*, he said to himself, *I know where I am, I think I'm standing in one of our fields overlooking Big Quill Lake.* "But why," he said out loud. Ayden turned his attention back to the lake where he saw a huge, white pelican take off from the water and land just meters from his feet. The bird was much larger up close than Ayden had expected, forcing the boy to take several, quick steps backwards. The bird walked toward him, then brought her wings to rest beside her body.

"Looks like you're ready to go to work," noted the pelican. Stunned by the fact that he could understand the bird, Ayden simply stared. "Hey buddy," said the bird taking a step closer, "You okay? Can you talk to me?"

"Uh," was all Ayden could say.

"No need to be scared. I see you have a hardhat on and I thought that meant that you were here to work." Immediately, Ayden's hands went to his head where, sure enough, he was still wearing the yellow hardhat from the Downtown Disney LEGO Store. Still not hearing a word from the boy, the pelican continued, "We've been expecting you. My name is Poppy. Yea, yea, I know Poppy the Pelican, I've heard all the jokes. I don't know what my mother was thinking when we were all hatched. My siblings are named Piper, Pippa, Petunia, Popeye, Pita and Cornelius... don't even ask!"

By now, Ayden was feeling a little more comfortable with the feathered creature. "What do you mean 'you've been expecting me'?"

"Just what I said. We heard through the grapevine that because of Disney Magic there would be help coming."

"Help for what?"

"To clean up the Quill Lake catastrophe."

"What!? You expect me to figure out how to fix THIS?" said Ayden as he pointed to the miles and miles of water in the distance. "My Dad said experts have been out here and THEY didn't know what to do."

"Of course, that's true, but then they didn't have you, or us, to help."

"Us?"

"Oh yes. Dozens and dozens of us woodland

creatures are standing by to help. This flooding has affected all of us and none of it in a good way. We want to help fix this enormous issue.

"I still don't get it," said Ayden shaking his head, now more bewildered than scared.

"There are some things you'll want to know. Number one - time is standing still for your parents and the rest of the world, so no one will miss you. Number two - all of this is happening in the blink of an eye so none of us will need to sleep or eat while we work. Number three - we will all be able to understand each other, no matter what species we are. Lastly, number four - if you look in the backpack you are carrying you'll see it contains most everything you will need to work with." Surprised he hadn't noticed the backpack before, Ayden slipped it off and opened the zipper. Inside, he found thousands of LEGO blocks. In fact, no matter how deep into the bag Ayden dug, he couldn't find the bottom. Just as he was about to show Poppy, she said, "Disney Magic, dude." All Ayden could do was shake his head and close the zipper.

"I'm not sure where to start," said Ayden.

"Do you know the problem?"

"I think so. My Dad told me the Quill Lakes have flooded way over their banks and destroyed lots of farmland. Because the water is so salty no one wants the extra water to go into their lake."

"Yep, that's about it, Ayden. We've heard you

are really smart and love to build things. That's why we know you can help us."

"Am I just supposed to sit right here and figure all of this out?"

"No," laughed Poppy. One of my friends has a home she wants to share with you while you come up with a plan."

"Really?" questioned Ayden, looking around and not seeing anyone else.

"Follow me and I'll take you there." Walking one behind the other, they eventually came upon a clump of brush and trees. Poppy pointed to the base of a rather large maple tree and gestured for Ayden to step closer.

"Yes, I see the tree, now what?" Poppy let out a loud whistle and within seconds, the base of the tree opened and a rather large raccoon peered out.

"Hey sweetie, how's my friend Rickrack today? I want you to meet Ayden."

"Is he...you know...the fixer...the builder...?"

"Yes! Here he is!" said Poppy proudly. Rickrack opened her door a little wider to get a good look at the human.

"Well, come in!" she invited. Ayden looked at the tree, the opening, then hesitated. *How would he and Poppy fit into a tree trunk,* Ayden wondered to himself. Poppy opened her wing slightly giving the boy a solid push from behind forcing him to stumble forward. He had to stoop down considerably to fit through the door but as he did, and his eyes adjusted to the dim light, Rickrack's home surprised him. Although the door was in the tree trunk the rest of the home was underground. There were several areas for sleeping, a room for relaxing and watching television and a room for eating.

"You can stay here as long as you need to, to plan."

"I don't even know what to plan, or how to plan it," admitted Ayden suddenly feeling lost.

"Don't worry dear, it will come to you," smiled the raccoon as she passed stacks of maps and papers towards the blonde-haired boy. Now, Ayden had never seen a raccoon up close. In fact, he had seen very few raccoons, they were night creatures, after all. Only once did he see one rummaging through a garbage bag that his Mom had left on their deck. But it had been dark and as soon as the animal saw Ayden it had scampered away. Right now, right there, in front of him, was a raccoon. He had to admit it was a nice-looking animal, mostly black and gray with kind of a cute face. Rickrack's dark, beady eyes were surrounded by black fur. Ayden had heard it called a mask and he thought it really did look like one, alright. He couldn't help but notice that when she spoke her delicate, gray whiskers that stuck out from both sides of her nose twitched. Her mid-section was quite plump and Ayden figured it was because of that that, she kind of waddled when she walked.

Her paws were what captured Ayden's attention the most. Although they were quite claw-like, with pads and nails, they resembled human hands which made it possible for Rickrack to pick up a pencil and hand it to the boy.

Chapter 4

Now what? thought Ayden to himself. He sat at the kitchen table with papers before him feeling overwhelmed. Slowly and gingerly, he reached for the one on the top of the stack. It still smelled of fresh ink, as if it had just been photocopied. How the raccoon managed to do THAT he really didn't want to know. Ayden continued to look through the papers. The more he looked, the more interested he became. After what seemed like several hours of examining photos and maps, his eyes felt tired. He looked up and stretched, then removed his glasses and rubbed his eyes with his fists. Things were a little blurry and the inside of Rickrack's kitchen was barely lit, but he was sure he could see multiple eyes looking at him from the shadows. He put his glasses back on then jumped, falling right off his chair. Indeed! There were many eyes staring right at him. He couldn't see their bodies only glowing red eyes of various sizes. Ayden lay on the ground for a second or two until he realized there was something underneath him. He looked down only to find a tail sticking out from under his leg.

"Squeal," went the creature.

"Aaaah," yelled Ayden, picking himself up in a hurry. The loud voices scared the once quiet animals who all began running for cover. Ayden peered down to discover the tail belonged to a tiny mouse. It was too stunned to move; his backside was sore and would show a bruise in the morning. Not knowing what to do, Ayden plunked himself back up on the chair, never taking his eyes off the mouse. When it didn't move except for a blink, Ayden reached down and gently cupped the gray creature in his hand. He stroked it softly feeling it shake with fear, its whiskers twitching furiously. "It's okay little fellow." The wide-eyed mouse took a deep breath and the shaking slowed. "Sorry about falling on you, are you hurt?"

"Just my butt, I'll be fine." Ayden stared in disbelief. I didn't expect you to talk to me and I didn't expect you to understand me, either."

"Yea, even though Poppy told you, we figured you'd be surprised at that. It's Disney Magic at work."

"Can I understand all of you?" asked Ayden of the many critters that were now reappearing from the shadows.

"Yes."

"Oh ya."

"Of course."

"Sure."

"Most definitely," were just some of the responses he heard while they all answered at once.

"Poppy was right. I CAN understand each and every one of you."

"Now that that is settled, back to work," insisted Rickrack. "We and many more creatures are ready to help." The multitude of animals slowly left the raccoon's den to attend to their own lives, giving Ayden the peace and quiet he needed to turn his attention back to the stack of information before him. He read reports that told him how salty the lakes were. He could see why it wasn't a good idea to put the salt water in a freshwater lake. He knew only certain kinds of animals could survive in salt water. So, if fresh water wasn't the place for the water to go then it had to go to a place where salt water already existed. It would have to be a large body of water to be able to handle the millions of gallons the Quill Lakes needed to get rid of. Ayden needed additional maps so he dug out his tablet and googled the information he wanted. It seemed, from his research, that the extra water needed to flow north, up to Hudson Bay which flowed into the Arctic Ocean. He didn't know how far the Quill Lakes were from the ocean but he knew it was a very long, long way. Now he needed an even bigger map. Again, his tablet was able to give him the distance between Big Quill Lake and the nearest point on Hudson Bay. It was a whopping 931 kilometers. He looked at the route the water would have to take. The straight line didn't look too bad on paper but Ayden knew that didn't mean a thing.

Now where do I start? Wondered Ayden to himself. As if reading his mind, Rickrack spoke, "You look worried."

"I am. I'm not sure what to do now. This is an enormous job. How can I do this?"

"I understand your worries," said Rickrack, "I want to remind you that many, many of my friends and relatives are on standby to help you, and don't forget we all have Disney Magic on our side."

"You're sure there is help for me?"

"Of course. Hundreds of creatures want to help. This overflow of lake water is causing major problems for us too. Many of my friends have lost dens because of the water. We are all anxious to get this problem fixed. Don't be surprised at how much help we will be."

Ayden began to take down some notes. He wrote down the number of kilometers the water would have to travel. He began looking up other information while keeping his fingers crossed. He relaxed a little when he found the data he had been looking for. The elevation of the Quill Lakes was higher than that of Hudson Bay. At least he would have gravity on his side. Ayden finally came up with a plan. It seemed easiest to dig a large, wide trench from one body of water to the other. It would be like making a new river.

Next, Ayden made a list of necessary equipment. He would need excavators to move dirt, other equipment like chain saws to cut down trees that stood in the way and graders to push dirt around. Surely there would be rocks in their way, so explosives and diggers with large buckets were added. He and his team would need to see what was ahead of them so he would need binoculars and maybe a drone.

His gaze turned to the backpack of endless LEGO. *Why would the Magic have given him those?* Then he remembered something Poppy had said to him. She had told him they heard he was good at building things. Was that the answer? Was he supposed to build what he needed out of LEGO? But LEGO blocks were just plastic, not steel or complicated like real machinery. But then there was the Magic... just maybe...

Ayden snatched the backpack, sat it up on the table in front of him and unzipped the main compartment. "First, I'll build something super simple just to see if it will work," said Ayden, out loud, to no one in particular. He quickly found the pieces he needed and his fingers had no trouble putting the blocks together just right. In no time, he had built a hand shovel that was ready to dig. He thrust the shovel into the bag of LEGO and scooped up as many as it would hold. The shovel remained in one piece despite the weight of the blocks. Ayden pulled the shovel out and tested it with something heavier, the dirt and rocks outside Rickrack's den. Sure enough, the shovel held together against the weight of those too. Ayden tried to pull the shovel's blocks apart but could not do it. It was as if all the pieces had been super-glued together. Now, he knew the Magic was real. He would have to use all the skills he had learned while putting together the dozens and dozens of LEGO kits he had built over the years. He had built everything from a Chinese boat, airport, airplanes, the Trevi fountain, machinery of all kinds and even a hockey rink. All of this experience would come in handy now.

Chapter 5

Ayden closed the maps, the tablet and tried to close his eyes. But everything that was rolling around in his head kept him from relaxing. He could sure use his Dad's help right about now but he knew his family was far away. A new sound startled the boy causing him to turn around and look behind him. A large, dark animal sat in the shadows. Ayden could not see it well enough to figure out what it was.

"Hello," said Ayden cautiously.

"Hi there. I've been wanting to meet you and you are finally here."

"Who are you?"

"I'm Slap. I'm a Canadian beaver. You know, we slap our tails."

"Why do you slap your tail?"

"It's our way of warning each other that danger is near."

"Oh, I guess I've heard about that. You also cut down trees and build dams, right?" asked Ayden, trying to remember what he had learned in school.

"You build dams!" repeated Ayden, the significance of the information finally sinking in. With renewed interest and energy, he asked, "Can you help me with this water problem?"

"Of course, you know one of our main jobs is to divert water, that's what dams do."

"How do you do that?"

"All beavers are born knowing something about it, but once we are old enough to chew down trees, we go to school to learn all about the physics and engineering of dam building and water diversion. I was thinking you could use me as your foreman or project manager. I know the area as well as many of the other animals. I think we would be a great team."

"I do need help. Let's work together." The beaver slapped his tail in excitement.

"Yes! Let's get 'er done!" Ayden smiled to himself thinking this was the expression he often heard his Uncle Tim use.

"So, how do we partner together?" asked Slap.

"I'll make up the overall plan and you make sure it is followed. My plan is to trench a river from Big Quill Lake to the southwestern part of Hudson Bay."

"Before you begin digging the new river, we will have to build a large dam in Quill Lake to hold the water back until you are ready to let it flow to Hudson Bay."

"Yes, that sounds good. The dam will have to be

very strong."

"We, beavers have the know-how so no problem. I'm going to have a meeting with the beaver union to see how many will be able to help us."

"A union? You know I can't pay any of you, right?"

"We don't expect to get paid. Fixing this problem will help us too. I'm going to the union just to get a list of beavers that can help. In the meantime, I'll tell other animals and recruit them too."

Ayden had an idea about how he would begin. It seemed logical to begin at the northern end of Big Quill Lake. He wasn't sure how deep he could dig. Was there rock below and, if so, how far beneath the surface? He needed some help and that help had to be able to dig. "I know! I need a gopher. They are great diggers. They have holes all over our yard." As if by magic (Disney Magic, of course), a gopher appeared jogging out of the tall grass towards the boy. *I better be careful about what I say out loud from now on,* thought Ayden.

"Hey," yelled Ayden to the approaching rodent.

"Hi, I'm Perry, I heard you call."

"I was thinking a gopher might be helpful because you can dig well."

"That's what we do best whether you want holes or not," boasted the little fellow. Ayden felt a pang of guilt as he remembered how he had watched his Dad put poison down the gopher holes in their yard. This little guy looked much cuter than the yard gophers. His golden-brown body was long and low to the ground. His back had a cool pattern of stripes which probably made him difficult to see in the grass, Ayden reasoned. He tried to put the poison out of his mind and focus on his new-found work friend. Percy interrupted his thoughts as he said, "Can you tell me just what you need to be dug?"

"We need to dig a channel for a river that will be over 900 kilometers long." Ayden hoped the size of the project would not discourage the small creature. But he soon found out the gopher wasn't bothered by the plan.

"Obviously, I can't do it alone."

"No, I wouldn't expect you to. I know that some other animals are great diggers too."

"For sure. I could see us teaming up with weasels, badgers and we can't forget the little guys like the moles and shrews."

"Can you all get along enough to work side by side? Ayden had a sneaking suspicion that some of the animals could be enemies.

"To be honest," said Perry, "some of us would be eaten by others but there is Disney Magic here so we will be able to be co-workers without any problems." With Ayden feeling confident that there would not be fighting among his work force, he began to put his plan in motion.

"The first thing I need you to do is to dig down until you hit rock. It's important that we know how deep we can dig the channel. The deeper, the better. Digging a test hole wasn't really necessary as far as Percy was concerned. He had been digging in Saskatchewan's dirt his whole life. He knew the many layers that made up the tiers from the top soil down to the bedrock.

"I'll gather the gang on the northern edge of the lake and we'll get to work," said Percy. Just to make sure Percy knew precisely where to start, Ayden pulled out a large map from its big, white tube and laid it carefully on a wide tree stump nearby, showing Percy the exact location. After a fist bump, the rodent scampered away with the plan in mind.

By the time Ayden made his way to the starting point, a large gathering of forest creatures could be seen hovering near the muddy lakeshore. The first shovel full would be special and Ayden and Slap would do it together, a ceremony of sorts. Ayden had put together a shovel made out of only yellow LEGO blocks and it sat nearby. Looking up, he saw Slap approaching with dozens of fellow beavers. "These are some of my union brothers and sisters. They are all willing to help with this flooding problem. I have explained to them what the goal is and together we are sure that you will find our help valuable." Ayden looked around at the dozens of animals that stood before them. He could hardly believe so many species lived so close to his home. From tiny shrews to massive deer, they were all gathered to work together to make their neighborhood a better place to live. With a little tear in his eye, he grabbed the shovel and stuck the tip into the thick, wet muck. With a smack of his tail, Slap pushed the shovel deep into the lakeshore, then Ayden lifted the shovelful of Quill Lake mud signifying the beginning of the end of the Quill Lakes catastrophe.

Chapter 6

The shovel was set aside and the animals began to organize themselves into work teams. Some would spend their time digging in the earth, some would stomp on the banks of the new river to prevent erosion, while others flew overhead helping to plot the route of the channel. Nine hundred kilometers was a long way and as the river was dug closer and closer to Hudson Bay, new, local work teams would take over, knowing their own neighborhoods best.

Slap and his cousin, Toothy, began to demonstrate to the teams in which direction the channel would be dug. "Now teams, digging should be easy here. We are in the Parkland region of the province. There are some trees and rocks but most of the soil is good, soft dirt."

"He is right," agreed Percy, who of course was a digging expert. When the first digging crew formed, its members included Percy, the gopher; Claw, the badger; Itsy and Bitsy, identical twin mice; Spike, the deer and Casey the Coyote. Those that could dig would move the dirt. Spike would use his hooves, strength and weight to move pesky stones and to tramp down the sides of the channel. Casey's strong jaw would pick up and carry rocks away. Piper and Petunia, sisters of Poppy the pelican would hover just high enough to ensure the channel was taking the proper route. But before any dirt could be moved, Toothy and his family jumped right in to the water to get a feel for its depth.

"Think you know how we should do this?" asked Chip, Toothy's son.

"Yes, I think, as a family, we can go ahead and start. We need a dam to keep the water out of the trench as it's being dug. Chip, you and Sawdust start cutting down trees. You know the kind. As many willow as you can find. Branch, you need to start pushing sand as a base. Once the guys have got a few trees on the ground, you need to cut the trunks into logs and place a post line across the channel. Then all of you can weave willow branches together."

"On it, Dad," yelled Branch.

"Just everyone, be careful," urged Bark, Chip's wife. The beaver family worked tirelessly building the dam. They didn't need to stop for a meal, but they had to keep their teeth worn down so they ate whatever was closest to them. They munched on inner bark, leaves and twigs of the willow trees that grew nearby. Mother beaver, Bark, brought down a small grove of aspen trees and dragged them to the family as a special treat.

Ayden was fascinated while watching the beaver family work. It was clear they had built many dams before. Their teamwork was amazing and the finished dam not only held back the water but looked like an engineering marvel. Now that the flow of the water was controlled, diggers could begin. Claw and Percy began digging furiously. They were very proud of the fact that they were the first to get the channel going. The difference in the animals' sizes soon became noticeable. It was no surprise that Claw could out dig Percy, yet both continued, encouraged by their animal neighbors, cheering them on.

Ayden's research had told him he needed to strengthen the sides of the channel. If he didn't, they would surely cave in and the water would not be able to flow. Lining both sides would have to be done before the beavers could release the water from behind the dam. Now Ayden knew why he had been given an endless supply of LEGO. He dumped a large pile of multicolored blocks into the freshly dug trench and proceeded to cover the sides in LEGO. As soon as the identical twin mice, Itsy and Bitsy saw what Ayden was doing they knew this was their task. The mice began hauling the blocks, one at a time, up the channel so larger animals could place them and interlock them for strength.

Poppy, the pelican who had been swimming on the lake hunting for food, soon took to the air gliding over the construction site. Once she figured out what was going on, she swooped in for a landing. "Hey Itsy and Bitsy, I think I can help you here."

"How is that?" asked Bitsy.

"Instead of moving one brick at a time like you, I can use this and haul hundreds at one." With that being said, Poppy opened her beak wide, showing the space below her jaw where she could hold about three gallons of water at once. Today, she would not fill it with water but instead would pack it full of LEGO blocks. "How about I load up then soar over the trench and let 'em fly?"

"You better watch out you don't hit Bitsy and I," cautioned the tiny mouse. She waggled her tiny finger at the giant bird and continued, "One wrong dump and Itsy and Bitsy will be Squishy and Squashy." Imagining what that would look like made Poppy's jaw drop. She certainly wouldn't want to hurt her miniature friends.

"Hey Rickrack," said Ayden, as he saw the raccoon ambling toward him.

"Hi boss, looks like you are off to a great start here. What can I do to help?"

"Right now, Percy has been doing the digging. Poppy is going to pick up the blocks and dump them on the sides of the trench, while Itsy and Bitsy arrange them. How about you help place them so they make a solid bank on both sides."

"Yep, I can do that but first I'm going to call for some backup."

"You mean more help?"

"Oh yea, I have plenty of family. Rickrack stood up on her hind legs, put her paw in her mouth and blew a piercing whistle, three longs and one short blast. Within a minute, six more raccoons came bounding through the prairie grass to the newly dug trench. The group was briefed on what to do when Bark, the beaver appeared. "I have an idea," she said, "Once you raccoons put the blocks on the banks, call us and we will come and slap them with our tails putting them very securely in place. They will never move."

"That's a great idea. Dig, drop, place and slap!" laughed Percy. "Sounds like teamwork to me."

"It sure does and I like it!" smiled the usually serious Ayden. And so, it continued, kilometer after kilometer, the deep, wide trench was dug, the sides covered with well-placed LEGO from the never-ending LEGO backpack. Slowly, the trench pointed northeast on its way to meet the Arctic Ocean as it flowed into Hudson Bay.

Chapter 7

The first town that the work crew came close to, was the small town of Porcupine Plain. Badger, Claw, Coyote Casey, Percy the gopher and Slap could just see the buildings in the distance when a chubby rodent came waddling towards them. Once the animals recognized what it was, they all hurried to get out of its way.

"No need to be frightened," said the good-natured fellow. "You would have to touch me to get hurt. Some think I can shoot my quills and they can fly, but that's ridiculous. I'm not a magician." And with that remark, the prickly dude roared with laughter at his own joke. Wiping the tears from his eyes he continued, "My name is Needles, but here in town they call me Quilly Willy, you know I'm the town mascot - Porcupine Plain - Quilly Willy." He tried to get some kind of reaction from the newcomers but none seemed particularly impressed. In fact, the only one who could think of something to say was Percy.

"So…you are the mascot of this tiny town are

ya? Well I have more exciting news than that! My cousin is the mascot for the Saskatchewan Roughriders, yes that's right! You ever heard of Gainer the Gopher? He's my cousin and he lives in the big city of Regina. Yes, he's my cousin alright, on TV every week, flies with the team to all their games, gets to hang out with the cheerleaders. He is a BIG shot and did I mention he's my cousin?"

"I think we get the picture, Percy," piped up Casey. Turning to the porcupine he said, "Nice to meet you Needles, I mean Willy. Thanks for coming out to cheer us on."

"Not much happens around here, so your project is big news. I think someone from one of the local papers may be around to interview the crew and take pictures."

"Here is the guy to be interviewed. It is his vision that we are all working to complete," said Casey, nudging Ayden forward with his nose. Ayden wasn't sure he wanted any publicity. He wasn't doing this to be famous, only to keep the salty water from ruining any more farmland. But sure enough, when the next edition of the <u>Hudson Bay Post Review</u> newspaper hit the presses, Ayden and his trench were featured on the front page.

❖❖❖❖❖   ❖❖❖❖❖   ❖❖❖❖❖

The work for the new salt water river was going well. The animals and Slap had placed them into informal teams that dug day and night. Some of the creatures saw better at night so they let other team members work during the day while they took over once the sun set.

As Ayden watched the progress the forest creatures were making, he couldn't help but notice how the landscape around him was changing. The small clumps of aspen, poplar and maple trees that towered over Saskatoon berry and chokecherry bushes near the Quill Lakes, gave way to more and more coniferous trees. The pines began to mix together with birch trees, both towering tall above the earth. Because of the growth of more trees, Ayden needed additional help. It would be best to avoid as many trees as possible so he needed someone, or something, to plot more of the river's course in advance. The beavers would surely help getting the trees out of the way but they were being kept busy strengthening the dam and slapping the LEGO blocks into solid structures along the river banks. What Ayden needed was more eyes in the sky like never before. Poppy and been very helpful but she and her sisters and brothers were back in Quill Lake attending to family matters.

Itsy, Bitsy, Casey and Percy had also gone home. They had passed their duties to friends and family who lived in a more northern part of Saskatchewan. Rickrack had cousins all over the place so she had had no trouble contacting a half of a dozen of them to take over. Stripes, Mask, Ringtail and Smoke began digging like raccoons do, while others waited their turn to take over, once dusk fell. They were joined by Percy's old high school gopher friend, Dirt. The smallest, and perhaps cutest, of the new crew was Minnie, the shrew.

"Hey everyone, I'm Dirt," declared the gopher. My old friend Percy said you could use some help digging."

"Hi Dirt," said Slap, "I'm the project manager here. I'm in charge of what gets done and who does it, and how. Our old crew went back home so it's time to find a new team of workers."

"You would be my boss, then," smiled Dirt.

"I guess you could say that, but even I have a boss and here he comes." Ayden could be seen walking in the distance toward the crew. "He is the brains here, I just get the workers to do what he wants."

"Wow!" said Dirt, with respect in his voice, "He figured all of this out?"

"Yes, to save the area around his home town of Wynyard. Ayden is a gifted boy. He is an expert at building with LEGO which has made him good at designing and constructing things." The four raccoons ceased digging with the approach of Ayden. Minnie, the shrew, however, continued shoving LEGO pieces into place.

"Hey Minnie," whispered Mask, "Get over here and meet Slap and Ayden."

"Get over where and meet who?" said Minnie,

her eyes squinted almost shut.

"You know...the bosses," insisted Mask.

"Oh yea," said Minnie. She scampered out of the trench and stood on the edge facing away from the beaver and the boy.

"What are you doing? Turn around. What are you, blind?"

"Yes, nearly blind," admitted the shrew. "My eyesight is terrible; all shrews have bad eyesight. We do all of our work at night so having sight isn't that important. But our hearing and smell work very well." By now, the shrew had turned and was facing Ayden. The conversation with Minnie made Mask think about how hard it would be if he didn't have good eyesight. He couldn't even begin to imagine.

"Good to meet you, Minnie and thanks for your help. You too Mask," said Ayden. "We do have a slight problem though. We need some help to keep looking ahead to help us decide where to dig next. We had a few pelicans helping us out but they had to return home."

"You mean like scouts?"

"Yes! That's just what we need."

"I know a guy that would be perfect for the job," said Ringtail. "My buddy, Hayden. He is a red-tailed hawk. He has fantastic sight and can soar miles above the ground."

"A hawk would be perfect!" said Ayden. "He could see way ahead and guide us. How can you find him?"

"He is easy to find. He will be sitting on top of a telephone pole or high up in a tree, always keeping a look out."

"When you find him, Ringtail, explain what we are doing and send him my way," said Ayden.

"I sure will!" As promised, Ringtail was able to locate Hayden without any trouble and several hours later, he landed a few feet from the human.

"Excuse me," Hayden called in a deep voice. I hear I could be of some help."

"Yes, yes, I am so glad to meet you," exclaimed Ayden, "Did Ringtail explain to you what is going on?"

"I think I understand what you need from me. You want someone to look forward to find a path for your new river. One that has the least number of obstacles in the way."

"We are hoping not to have to go around too many things although there seems to be a lot of trees and more rocks here than down south."

"There are a lot of trees here and there will be even more the further north you go. I find it quite funny when I hear people say Saskatchewan is flat and barren."

"I'm not surprised at how it looks," said Ayden. "My family stays in a cabin each July and the land around it looks just like this. Well, enough chatter, let's get started. How about you take a look from high in the clouds, then we can get together and continue to make our map?" suggested Ayden.

"Hmm, I think I have a better idea. One of my best friends is Phil. He is a proud bald eagle. How would you like to get a bird's-eye view for yourself? Phil is huge. I think you could sit on his back and fly with him. How does that sound?"

"Terrifying!" blurted out Ayden. He felt both excited and scared to death. On one hand, it would be the opportunity of a lifetime, plus he could see first-hand, where to trench next. Yet, on the other hand, how could he fly hundreds of feet in the air without falling off?

"I know what you're thinking. But I can assure you Phil would keep you very safe. Come on Ayden, I can get a message to him via flymail."

"Flymail? What is that?"

"We don't use email or the post office so we rely on flymail. I fly a few miles and give the message to a bird buddy of mine, then she flies off till she meets a friend. She tells her friend the message who flies off, and so on. Eventually, the message will be delivered to Phil."

"I guess we could try it,"

"Okay, here we go. Tell Phil to meet us at the southwest part of the forest." And with that Hayden flew away. Several miles later the hawk came across his buddy, Checker, a black and white magpie.

"Hi Checker, I'm trying to get a message to Phil by using flymail. I'm hoping you can help."

"Sure, what's the message?"

"Phil is to meet the work crew at the southwest part of the forest."

"Here I go."

"Thanks, buddy." Checker had flown a dozen or so miles when he saw a familiar pair of wings up ahead. It was his old friend, Carla, the crow.

"Carla, hey Carla. Wait up."

"Oh my gosh! Is that you, Checker?"

"Yes, it's me. I'm helping a good friend get a message to Phil via flymail. Could you help me out?"

"You know I will. What's the message?"

"Phil is to sneak the work crew into the southwest part of the forest."

"Sneak what work crew?"

"I don't know, I didn't ask. I just promised I would deliver the message."

"Well, okay, I'll be on my way then." And with many questions still rattling around in her mind due to the strange message, Carla took flight. Barely eight miles had gone by when a large bird loomed up ahead. It was a hawk, in fact it was Jack. Jack and Carla had been friends since they had been hatched. "Jack, Jack, it's me, Carla. How are you?"

"Oh, my goodness, I haven't seen you in a long time."

"It's been a while. I don't have time to chit chat. I'm on a mission. I'm wondering if I can ask you to get a message to Phil.

"I'll help the best I can. What's the message?"

"He is to sneak the work stew into the southwest forest."

"Work stew? I've never heard of that and why would it have to be snuck into the forest?"

"Don't ask me. I'm just the message deliverer," sighed Carla.

"Well, I'm off. I should be able to track down Phil," said Jack. He wasted no time in taking off, flying just above the tree tops in search of the large eagle. It was hard to say exactly where he would be, but Jack knew to look for his nest. It would be built high in a very sturdy tree. The hawk flew over the forest zig-zagging back and forth until he saw what was surely a nest belonging to a very large bird. Jack was smart enough not to land in the nest. Eagles were territorial and they could be vicious if thought they were under attack. Instead, Jack landed in a neighboring tree and call out to Phil.

"Hey, Phil, you there, ole buddy?" Immediately, a bald head popped up, but it wasn't Phil.

"He's not here right now," said the eagle, "He's on a screech audition."

"A what?"

"An audition. He found out that the screeches hawks make are often used in movies and on television to sound like raptors. He figured if hawks could be hired so could eagles. What do you need him for? I'm his wife, by the way."

"Pleased to meet you. My name is Jack and I promised to get an important message to Phil."

"I can give him the message; what is it?"

The message is "Phil is to peek into the pork stew in the southwest forest."

"Peek into the pork stew?"

"Yea, I know. I don't get it either, but that's the message."

"Maybe it's in code. Whatever, I'll give it to him." Just then, Phil's wife was interrupted by one of her fledglings and pounced back into her nest, a sure sign that their conversation had ended. Jack flew off, satisfied that he had been able to find Phil's nest and deliver the message.

Phil eventually returned to his nest and received the strange communication. He had no idea what it meant so he left the nest in search of the smartest bird he knew, Snowflake, the owl. Everyone called her Flake. It was dusk now, and Phil knew Flake would be waking up, ready to begin her nightly quest for food. He also knew where her hunting ground was and felt sure he would find her there. After soaring high above the tree tops, he spotted something dazzling white sitting atop a tall lodgepole pine tree. He lowered his altitude to get a better view. Once the owl looked up he knew he had found his friend.

"Flake! Hey, Flake, I've been looking for you," yelled Phil, as he settled on a nearby branch.

"Good to see you, Phil, how are you doing?"

Flake asked as they slapped wings in a sort of high five.

"I won't waste time cause I know you're hungry, but I've come to pick your brain."

"Pick my brain?" screeched Flake as she jumped further away from Phil.

"I'm not here to really pick your brain, what I mean is I'm here to ask you to help me solve a strange message. Your the smartest bird I know."

"Oh, that's different. What is the message and whooo sent it?"

"I understand the message came to me by flymail. I don't know who started it. The message has been flown throughout the forest by various birds until it got to me. The message I received is 'peek into the pork stew at the southwest forest.'"

"That doesn't make much sense," remarked the wise bird.

"You're telling me."

"Let's see if we can figure this out together. Do you know what pork stew is?"

"Not a clue."

"Well, at least we know where the southwest part of the forest is. I think we should go there and see if that gives us any hints."

"You're willing to come too?"

"Yes I am. I'm intrigued now. I have to find out what's going on." The two birds leapt off their tree limbs flying in a southwesterly direction hoping to find the pork stew... whatever that was!"

Chapter 8

The two strong birds wasted no time in making their way to the designated area of the forest. While Phil was gliding most of the way because of his amazing wide wingspan, Flake stayed much closer to the ground so she could swoop down and catch the dinner and dessert that Phil was helping her track.

Even before the edge of the forest came into view, the two birds could feel something unusual was happening on the ground. It seemed that many of the forest creatures were gathered at the edge of the woods. Still partially hidden by the brush and tree limbs, it was clear the group was watching and listening to a human! They were with a human!

"Whatever is going on down there?" asked Phil, out loud.

"I don't know but humans aren't often seen in this part of the forest and when they are, they usually mean trouble. Do you think he has something to do with your message?"

"I'll bet he does!" said a surprised Phil, beginning to swoop towards the ground.

"Whoa, whoa, there fella,' cautioned Flake, "You don't know what he is up to, and look, he has a bunch of creatures around him. I say we do a couple of fly-bys to try to figure out if it's safe to land."

"Good idea, I didn't think of that," admitted Phil. And that's exactly what they did. Each time they flew by Ayden and his crew, they dipped lower and lower.

Hayden was the first to spot the soaring pair, "Hey, that's my buddy, Phil, up there," he said, pointing upwards with his large wing. "He's the better idea I was telling you about." Ayden looked towards the sky and noticed a snow-white owl and a very large bald eagle swooping towards him. Instinctively, he hit the ground, expecting the birds to strike.

"Get up, Ayden," Hayden managed to get out while laughing hysterically. No one is going to attack you." Hayden began flapping his wings as a signal for his friend to land. Just as Hayden flew onto a low branch, the eagle and the owl glided to a stop right beside him.

"Phil! You must have got my message, it's sure good to see you."

"Good to see you too, Hayden. This is my old friend, Snowflake.

"Hi Snowflake."

"Hi Hayden, everyone calls me Flake."

"Hayden, neither Flake nor I could figure out your message."

"I don't know why not. It's pretty clear. What part confused you?"

"The part where it says, 'peek into the pork stew in the southwest forest'. I knew where the southwest part of the forest was but would somebody please tell me what the heck pork stew is and how am I supposed to peek at it!" Hayden nearly fell off his branch backwards he was laughing so hard. Tears began to dribble down his cheeks as he tried to tell Phil what the message was supposed to be. He knew flymail could be unpredictable and this proved it. He was lucky Phil had decided to come at all.

"No, no, the message was, 'come meet the work crew in the southwest forest.'" After hearing the real message, Phil and Flake both joined in Hayden's amusement. That was the problem with flymail alright. Now that the message was clear, Hayden began to tell Phil his plan. First, he explained to the two birds who Ayden was and what he was hoping to accomplish. Then, he asked Phil if he could fly with Ayden on his back to scout locations for the river. Before Phil could answer, Flake interrupted the conversation.

"I suppose Phil could act like a carrier pigeon, but I think I have a much better and safer solution. Not only will it keep Ayden off an eagle's back, where he belongs, but it should hasten the entire project. Without another word, Snowflake disappeared.

By now, Ayden had walked over to the tree where the birds sat. "Ayden, this is my buddy, Phil, he is a bald eagle." Ayden had never seen such an enormous bird. The white feathers of the eagle's head stood out next to his piercing yellow eyes. Phil's beak looked very powerful and dangerously sharp. His dark brown body was thick and muscular, much like his legs. The most dangerous part of this bird had to be his feet with their razor-sharp talons and claws. Ayden had heard that eagles were so strong and powerful they could glide down and easily grab a lamb, goat, other small animal, even a dog. He could probably grab a small boy too, thought Ayden, beginning to tremble a little. He decided to play it cool and simply replied,

'Hi, Phil." Phil extended his enormous wing and gave Ayden a little tap on the back, reassuring the boy he wasn't there to harm him. "Phil seems like an unusual name for an eagle."

"I know, right. It is. My Dad is a Philadelphia Eagles fan, so that's where the name came from, Phil is short for my real name, Philadelphia."

"I guess I should consider myself lucky. My Dad is a Miami Dolphins fan and I should be relieved that he didn't name me Flipper!" The birds and the boy had a great laugh over Ayden's joke.

Where did the white bird go?" asked Ayden.

"I have no clue, but she said she had a good idea. She's an owl after all and they say owls are very wise. So, let's wait and see what she does." In the meantime, Ayden introduced Phil to the crew that had stopped work near the edge of the forest. Phil was impressed to meet Ringtail, Mask, Smoke, Stripes, Dirt, Minnie and of course, Slap.

"That's quite a bunch you have helping you."

"The animals have been amazing helpers. We couldn't have gone this far without them."

"You are in our territory, our homes, so it was a good idea that you had the local creatures help. After all, they know their own region best."

"That's exactly what I thought and Slap, the project manager, has been a big help getting them to agree to work, then helping them to organize into work crews."

Just as Ayden and Slap were about to discuss the need to find more scouts, they heard a faint "whooo, whooo, whooo." It seemed the voice was coming from above and when they looked up they saw the beautiful white bird coming in for a landing. Then, they heard some unfamiliar sounds. Whirr, whirr, whirr was coming from the sky but the only thing Ayden could see were clouds. The noise of a loud engine could also be heard and it sounded like it was coming from inside the forest but all anyone could see were the trees. Other loud, peculiar noises were swirling all around the group and many of the forest animals began taking cover. All at once, the sources of the mysterious sounds came into view, almost causing Ayden to faint! The first surprising sight was a large blue and black helicopter whirling just over the tops of the trees. It moved slowly over the tops of the pines then slowly sank out of sight. Just as Ayden was about to start asking questions, Flake landed beside him.

"Ayden, I have a few things to show you. Follow me into the forest. I think you will like what you see." Stunned by the presence of the familiar-looking helicopter, Ayden, silently, did what he was told. As Flake flew from branch to branch, Ayden followed with Slap right behind him. If Ayden had been paying attention, he would have noticed many of the forest creatures had scampered ahead to find out the mystery. But he was too anxious to notice much around him. After tramping through the bush, he came to a large clearing. What he saw there had to be a dream.

"Slap, would you please slap me with your tail?"

"Slap you with my tail? Have you gone crazy? Why would I do that?"

"To wake me up, I'm sure I'm dreaming."

"No, my friend, you are not dreaming unless I am part of your dream too because I can see it too." By now, Phil had caught up and was circling high overhead. He had never seen anything like this before. He needed to get closer to the ground, closer to Flake. She would have all the answers. Finally, Flake quit flying and hopped over to the human.

"What do you think, Ayden?"

"I, I don't know what to think," admitted Ayden. "I know what all of these machines are!"

"Of course, you do. You better know. You built them!"

"You mean these are actually mine?"

"Right off your bedroom shelves. By the way, dusting them once in a while wouldn't hurt, you know."

"But how did...how could... how in the heck," stammered Ayden, shaking his head from side to side.

"You're not the only one that knows how to use Disney Magic. Why not use all these great machines you have already built? We will still need the animals for many things but the heavy work should be done by machines that are designed to do it. They made a great display in your room but we need to put them to work."

"Wow!" was all Ayden could manage to say. He remembered building each and every one of the LEGO kits. He had been building LEGO for years. It was one of the things he liked doing the most with his Dad. Sometimes, he and his sisters, Mya and Alyxa would build with the LEGO that filled multiple drawers and bins in their home, as well.

The helicopter had already landed at the LEGO

hangar. Next to the hangar, he could just make out the gas barrel, two jets and a good old-fashioned prop plane. Off to the right, was the Scarecrow's harvester with its rotating cutters. It was meant to be operated by an evil being but Ayden had no trouble comprehending how it could help them in the forest. Far above the hangar, the planes and other equipment, Ayden caught a glimpse of what looked like a towering crane in the distance. All of this had been so surprising and amazing. What a genius idea Snowflake had had. He was sure their work would progress faster now.

Chapter 9

As Ayden, Slap and the other forest creatures walked closer to the hangar, the boy thought he could see some folks he recognized. Crawling out of the helicopter were Claw and Casey. It was a good feeling to see someone from his own neighborhood. Ayden took off running toward the newcomers, anxious to ask them a million questions about how they got to the northern forest. As soon as the Coyote and the badger spotted Ayden, they came running towards him too, full of their own questions.

"Oh, Casey and Claw, what are you both doing here?"

"That big, snowy owl dropped by and asked us if we would help you again. Then she said it involved flying!" screeched Casey.

"I had never flown before," said Claw, "I couldn't pass up the opportunity for a new experience. But then, I saw what she meant by flying. It was a little helicopter no more than maybe eight inches long and six inches high."

"Yes, but it was very cool. It had six blades on it, some guns on the sides and a Batman symbol on the front. I wasn't passing that up," interrupted Casey.

"I turned around to look at Casey and when I turned back, the aircraft had grown to the size of a real chopper. I almost peed my pants it scared me so bad."

"How did Flake do it?" asked Ayden.

"Don't worry, I asked her that right away. All she would say was 'whooo, whooo, whooo knows'. She told us to get in, so we did and then Rickrack got in the pilot seat and flew us here."

"That's amazing. Wait! Where is Rickrack now?"

"Couldn't tell you, more mystery, I guess."

"What, or who, is that over there?" Ayden could see a small being near the hangar.

"I don't know, I didn't see anyone else there when we landed. Look! I see another plane. It wasn't there a minute ago." Sure enough, sitting inside the hangar was a plane with a large propeller. Running from it towards the group was a striped gopher.

"Percy!" yelled Ayden, "buddy, how did you get here?" Before Percy could answer, Ayden had already prepared himself for any crazy explanation the gopher might have. So far, not much had made sense.

Percy began to answer. It was clear he was worked up because his explanation came fast and furious, "I was digging a new hole when a gigantic, white owl flew over me. It scared me to death, owls enjoy eating gophers, you know. I dug even faster, so I could have a place to hide. Finally, the hole was big enough for me to crawl into so I stayed there for a long time just to make sure the owl had gone to look for a different meal. When I came out, she was sitting right there on the ground. I was sure I was a goner, but then she spoke to me. Once she mentioned your name, I figured out she wasn't there to eat me after all, and she wasn't. She offered me a chance to fly a plane up here to the forest. I told her gophers don't leave the ground, let alone fly planes. Heck, we don't even drive cars but then she told me that once I got in the plane I would know how. I laughed at her because, well, first of all, the plane wasn't big enough to even hold a shrew. But then, right before my eyes the plane grew and grew until it was just my size. I climbed into the cockpit and sure enough, I knew just what to do. I flew here, and landed the plane right in front of the hangar. I was just climbing out when I saw you!" And with that long, loud and fast explanation, Percy keeled over onto the ground gasping for air, trying to catch his breath.

"You okay, Percy?"

"Oh yea, yea, just winded, give me a moment."

"That's an incredible story, Percy, and if I hadn't already saw what I've already seen today, I wouldn't have believed a word of it! Ayden gently lifted his friend up off the ground then gave him a hug.

"Anyone ready to get back to work?" asked Slap, as he put his hardhat back on his head.

"Yes, let's get going," agreed Ayden.

"Now that we have a way of getting above the trees, how about we ask Claw and Casey to take us for a ride," suggested Slap.

"I'm certainly ready to see what's up ahead," agreed Ayden. Casey and Claw climbed into the chopper behind the controls while Ayden and Slap took the back seats and put on the provided headsets. Up, up they flew until they were high above the trees, then the pair flew them in a northeasterly direction looking for the best place to dig next. They flew for miles over dense forest until they came to a clearing where a town was sitting on the edge of a large lake, fed by three rivers.

"This might be a good place to think about trenching," said Slap, "Because the land has already been cleared, it would make it a little easier for us."

"What town is this?" asked Ayden.

"This is Cumberland House. The oldest settled community in Saskatchewan. It dates back to the 1700's when it was a very important trading post set up by the Hudson Bay Company."

"The Hudson Bay?" My Mom shops at that store in Saskatoon."

"Yes, it's the same store but it doesn't buy beaver pelts anymore. Thank heavens!" said Slap, smoothing down his fur lovingly. He continued, "The Cree and the Chipewyan helped settle the area. Some pretty important people in history once used this settlement. You might not recognize the names of Frobisher or La Vérendrye but they are famous in North American history."

"From what I can see, you are probably right, we should dig the water trench near here." Work began again through the forest near the settlement. Ayden had been correct; the Scarecrow's harvester was an enormous help. It cut down bush, tall grass, brush and saplings with its wide, rotating blades leaving a clean path for the digging to begin. Rickrack had gone from airplane pilot to harvester driver and she loved every minute of it. At about that time, Ayden wished he had built some sort of back hoe but then he remembered he had! Well, it wasn't exactly a digger but it was a machine that could move heavy things. He was sure it would come in handy. Now, it was time for the little critters to get busy again.

Joining Percy, the gopher, Claw the badger and Casey the coyote, were some new diggers. The new crew included large and small animals, each with an important task. The chief diggers were now Jaw, a wolverine, Sly, the fox, and another great digger, Dot who was Minnie, the Shrew's cousin. The work crew was standing together awaiting their instructions when Ayden and Slap appeared. The bosses walked up behind Dot who immediately fell to the ground, clearly unconscious. "Oh my," exclaimed Ayden, "What is wrong with her?"

"Nothing," replied Sly, "In case you didn't know, shrews are very nervous creatures. The smallest of scares can make them faint." Don't worry, she'll come to in a moment." As if Sly's words worked magic, by the time the words came out of his mouth, Dot was back on her feet as if nothing had happened. Figuring the tiny rodent was fine, Ayden ignored the unfortunate episode and carried on with his instructions.

Everyone got busy digging the channel and placing the LEGO blocks on the banks of what would be the new river. Rickrack went first, making sure there was a clear path and the diggers followed. As the crew crept further and further along, Rickrack would leave her harvester long enough to pilot the chopper so Slap and Ayden could see where the river might go. From their bird's eye view, they could see a fairly large town looming up ahead and Ayden knew the river should bypass the town, once again taking advantage of the area that had already been cleared of forest.

"Put us down," Slap instructed. "Let's check out this area."

"Boss," said Slap, "According to the map, we just crossed the Saskatchewan-Manitoba border.

That would make this town Flin Flon."

"Now, that's a weird name for a town. Actually, it's a weird name for anything."

"Yes, it is. I heard the town was named after a character from a science fiction story." The helicopter began to slow down and make its descent. It maneuvered around a bend before gently sitting on the ground outside of town next to a few scraggly trees surrounded by rock.

Oh, boy! Look at all these rocks. That's going to slow us down, said Ayden to himself. A look to his left made Ayden gasp. Sitting like it had been there forever, was his hangar. Somehow, it had been moved further north, once again. Ayden wondered how that had happened but then figured it was just one more thing that couldn't be explained.

Out of the landscape, came two large, black figures. Slowly, they ambled towards the human and his helpers. The closer they got, the more nervous Ayden became. It didn't take him long to recognize that the figures belonged to black bears.

"Hi Ayden, we heard you were coming, Flin Flon welcomes you. I'm Char and this is Coal."

"Hi and thanks," answered Ayden, "We won't interfere with your town, we will do our digging far enough away. We started digging at Big Quill Lake in Saskatchewan and we will end our project at Churchill, Manitoba."

"The Canadian Shield will make digging slow going, its solid bedrock."

"Our crew is concerned about that," admitted Slap.

"Let's walk over to our hangar," suggested Ayden, who had already spotted a new piece of equipment. "Look, Slap, it's my excavator that has the hammer arm. That should be able to help us break up the rock so it can be hauled away."

"I'm excited, that's exactly what we need." Once again, Ayden chose to ignore the magic that had brought this newest piece of equipment to them. He remembered building it with his Dad years before. It had sat high on a shelf opposite his bunk bed. Just like the other building projects they were using, it had grown from toy to life size.

"Look," said Char, pointing with her paw, "Here comes Max." Ayden followed the stare of the bear and saw an enormous, gangly moose walking slowly towards them. Now, the only thing Ayden knew about moose was that they were huge, and often got in the way of vehicles on the highway near his house. He had also read that they could be very mean. This more than worried Ayden, and Slap wasn't so sure of the creature either.

"Howdy Max, how've you been?" asked Coal.

In a very deep, slow-speaking voice, the giant creature answered, "Pretty good, pretty good."

"Are your goggles new? I don't think I remember seeing you wearing them before."

"Yes, thanks for noticing. As you know, moose have terrible eye sight and our faces are often underwater when we eat water plants. The other day I swallowed a pop can and half of a broken fishing rod before I figured out they weren't food. That's when I got glasses but then I figured I may as well get them made into goggles for underwater vision. How do they look?"

"You look very distinguished with them on and how they hook onto your antlers is pure genius," offered Coal.

"Why thanks. I'm here to help this crew however I can."

"Good eyesight will come in handy for this job," remarked Ayden, relaxing a little next to the giant. "I'm Ayden and this is my project manager, Slap."

"Good to meet you sir," said Max, bowing his head in respect.

"You might be good at running our excavator," suggested Slap.

"I'd like that, it looks like a really cool machine." Max climbed inside the large cab and drove it out of the hangar to the job site, where he sat ready to bust up some rocks!

Slap took the walkie talkie off his belt and spoke into it, "Okay, crew, the excavator and hammer are ready to go. Let's do this!"

"Roger that," replied a tiny voice. Ayden remembered that the walkie talkies had come with his hangar kit and were sure coming in handy now.

Chapter 10

The work through the Canadian Shield was much slower than it had been through the forest. On and on, kilometer after kilometer, the crew labored. Max stayed ahead of everyone breaking up the rock, local caribou loosened the rock pieces with their strong hooves and antlers so the crane could move them out of the way. Magically, the backpack of LEGO remained full despite the tens of thousands of blocks that had been used along the miles of trench already dug. The forest creatures remained dedicated to the job of allowing a new river to flow.

Many kilometers northeast from Flin Flon, the crew found themselves in the middle of the tundra with no cities, no town, no villages or even settlements nearby. For a change, Flake climbed into the chopper to do some scouting. After a long while, she radioed the ground saying she could finally see a rather large town up ahead. According to the map, it had to be Thompson, Manitoba.

"Come pick me up Flake, I want to see this

place," said Ayden. Flake sat the chopper softly down allowing Ayden and Slap to climb aboard. The three flew for quite a while when buildings shot up out of the tundra. It was a good size town and it surprised Ayden that so many people lived this far north. They flew right over the settlement and Ayden began to recognize some familiar-looking buildings. He could see schools with their playground equipment, churches with their tall spires, the local fire station, the courthouse and a very long building with a Zamboni parked behind it. Of course, it was the town's skating and hockey arena. Every town on the prairies had one of these. The helicopter continued to fly low over the town when something caught Ayden's attention, out of the corner of his eye. "Can you set us down nearby. I want to get a closer look?"

"Of course," said Flake.

"Look over there," said Ayden pointing out the side window of the helicopter. It was a large building with a gigantic wolf painted on the side of it. Ayden, and his travelling companions, scrambled out of the chopper to get a better look at the biggest piece of art they had ever seen. Just as the trio was admiring the mural, a loud voice came from behind, causing them all to jump. Ayden quickly turned around, startled. What he saw certainly matched the voice he had heard. It was a wolf! Everyone knew about wolves, they were vicious, ferocious meat eaters that travelled in packs making them very efficient hunters. Ayden, Slap and Flake were all made up of meat, perfect snacks for the creature. The boy and the beaver backed away without taking their eyes off the wolf's mouth while Flake flapped her wings and flew straight to the top of a tall pole. All of them were hoping this guy's pack hadn't surrounded them.

"Do you like the painting?" the wolf asked," it's of me, you know."

"I love it," whispered Ayden.

"Welcome to Thompson, Manitoba, my name is Mackenzie, my friends call me Mack."

Still unsure of the large dog-like creature, Ayden answered, "Thanks, my name is Ayden, this is Slap and that white owl over there is Snowflake. We are building…"

"I know what you are building, in fact everyone, for miles, knows what you are doing. I only came to introduce myself and welcome you to our city." Relief spread over Ayden's face, he smiled as he thanked Mackenzie and motioned to Flake to fly back and meet their host. Obviously proud of his city, Mackenzie continued "This is the wolf capital of the world. The people here think of us as their ancestors did. The indigenous people, mainly the Cree Indians lived here hundreds of years ago. They considered us as equals, as brothers."

"Wow! I didn't know any of that," piped up Slap, happy that he wasn't going to be on Mackenzie's dinner plate tonight.

"It looks like your digging is going well," commented Mack.

"We started digging in the Canadian Shield back in Flin Flon, it's been a little slower since then."

"This part of the world is billions of years old," Mack reminded them.

"It's different looking than where we live. Here, there are no farms or fields. All we can see from the air is tundra, trees and water."

"You are right. There isn't much soil here, just tundra."

"No farming at all, so how do people make a living?"

"Lucky for us, in northern Manitoba, there are valuable things to mine. Further north there is uranium, gold, silver and even diamond mines. Some of the people who live here, work in those mines."

"Gold and diamonds!?" exclaimed Ayden, with excitement.

"Oh yes," continued Mack, "Canada produces excellent quality ores and diamonds. We have a museum in our town that shows how they are mined. A good friend of mine runs it, would you care to take a look?"

"I sure would," said Ayden. His Mom would love to know more about gold and diamonds, two of her favorite things. Ayden accompanied Mackenzie to the museum where he was given the grand tour. At the end of the visit, the museum manager gave

Ayden two incredible gifts. A piece of rock that contained a raw diamond and a small nugget of real gold. Both were put in a small plastic bottle for safe keeping and Ayden placed them deep in his pants pocket.

It was time for the work crew and their bosses to continue moving forward with their job. The next settlement would be the city of Churchill, on Hudson Bay! Knowing they were getting close to their final destination encouraged all of the work teams to approach their job with renewed energy, the end was near! Far in the distance, there seemed to be a cluster of buildings. It just had to be Churchill. Percy took the helicopter up one more time to take a look. He could hardly wait to land and tell Ayden the good news. It was the edge of Hudson Bay. As the crew continued to dig, they were excited to not only see the city but also the shoreline. Ayden didn't know much about Churchill except that it had polar bears and he was very excited to meet one. He didn't have to wait long. Just like the other communities they had worked near, the city had its own welcoming committee and of course, it was made up of polar bears.

The bears walked directly toward Ayden and Slap. The closer they got, the knot in Ayden's stomach became tighter. He didn't think he should be afraid, but these creatures were gigantic. The white animals stopped several meters away.

"You must be Ayden," the first bear said. Ayden couldn't help but notice the enormous teeth in the bear's mouth and the claws on its four paws. He had seen them in a zoo once and had read how deadly they could be.

"Yes, I am. How did you know we were here? We are still so far away from town."

"Haha, that's funny. We can smell our prey from 35 kilometers away. We knew you were coming a long time ago." Ayden swallowed hard, he heard the word 'prey' and he didn't like it. The other bear began to laugh so hard that his belly shook.

"Look, Nanook, I think he's afraid of us."

"I think you're right," roared Koda, the first bear. "Are we right?"

"I'm a little scared. You are both so huge and I've heard polar bears can be vicious."

Again, both bears laughed out loud. "That's what we like to hear," said Koda, as he and Nanook high-fived each other.

"Wait," said Ayden trying to understand what the bear had just said. "You want us to think you're mean?"

"Of course. We are a big deal up here because of our reputation and we want to keep it that way."

"Really? What do you do so people think you are mean?"

"Lots of things. Like on Hallowe'en night, we remind the people of the town to patrol the streets with guns so it looks like they are protecting the little trick or treaters from us. We aren't interested in eating kids, give me a break."

"We really don't have any enemies, except guns, of course."

"If people think you are friendly you don't think tourists would want to come and see you. Is that it?" asked Slap.

"Yes, that's right. People want to see the huge, ferocious polar bears up close and if they thought we were gentle, we wouldn't be such a big deal."

"Did you know that the principal of the elementary school keeps a rifle in his office? He keeps it there just in case visitors come to visit him, so he can explain why he needs a gun. He tells them it's in case we come onto the playground," said Koda.

"The principal knows us. He knows we have no reason to come to school. We graduated years ago and we have our own educational system for our cubs."

"We especially like fall when thousands of tourists come here to ride terrain buggies to get a close-up look at us. We put on a really good show. After all, we want folks to get their money's worth."

"It's pretty cool around here when there are lots of tourists. My photo was posted on Facebook and Koda's picture has been on some advertisements both on television and Churchill's website. We're celebrities!"

Ayden had been listening intently, amazed at what he had heard. "So, you don't eat people?"

"No, of course not. Way too fatty for us, not at all healthy. We do enjoy the occasional seal and of course reindeer are delicious. The only problem with reindeer is they can see us against the snow because they have special eyes, making them very hard to catch."

"We like being the center of attention around here. Who doesn't want to be a celebrity, right Nanook?" said Koda, elbowing his buddy.

"We will do our best not to interrupt your tourist trade," assured Slap. "We are almost finished with our project. All we have to do is extend the trench to the bay."

"We will let you get back to work then," said Koda.

"Good to meet you both," replied Ayden. While the bears lumbered slowly back toward the town, the crew continued their work to the ocean.

In no time, the last digging effort reached the shore. What a wonderful feeling it was to feel the icy water on their hands and paws. Although the long trench was completed, no water had been allowed to flow from the Quill Lakes. The last obstacle was the large beaver dam that Slap and his family had built at the start of the trench. Now, it was time to break it apart. Flake sat behind the helicopter's controls while she flew to pick up Slap.

Once buckled in, she flew the beaver back to the hangar. There, Percy was waiting to fly Slap back to Quill Lake in the antique plane.

A large crowd had gathered at the dam site and another had gathered at Hudson Bay. The beavers wasted no time in tearing apart their well-made dam. They watched, amid cheers, as the salty water from the Quill Lakes spilled into the trench sloshing its way toward the ocean. The water began to flow in a northerly direction. But how would they know if there were any leaks in the new river? If there were, it would defeat the purpose of the whole project. Leaky salt water would leach into the good soil, contaminate it and make it impossible for plants to grow and for animals to drink it or live in it. It would be vital to take a look at the entire river, all 931 kilometers of it. Ayden reached for his walkie-talkie and spoke to his project manager, "Slap, we must make sure the river is sound. I'm leaving this job to you buddy."

"Yes, boss," answered the beaver. Slap knew just how to make the river inspection happen. He knew who he could count on and who had the expertise. After some time, a loud cheer went up in the northern community of Churchill as a steady stream of water gurgled right into Hudson Bay. They had done it! Along with millions of gallons of water, Ayden could see a speck of blue in the distance. What the heck was bouncing along, way out there? Casey could see the questioning look on his boss's face so he handed Ayden a pair of binoculars. Instantly, the speck in the distance became recognizable. It was the LEGO tug boat he had built years ago. The closer the boat came, the more excited Ayden felt. On the roof, the forward deck, the aft deck, the starboard and port rails were many of the creatures from the Quill Lake area.

◆◆◆◆◆   ◆◆◆◆◆   ◆◆◆◆◆

The bright sun glistening on the water, caused Ayden to blink and when he opened his eyes he was standing in front of the gigantic bulldozer outside of the LEGO store in downtown Disney. His Dad had just taken his picture.

"Don't forget to leave the hardhat here," reminded Dad. Dazed for a second, Ayden removed the hat and placed it on the stool next to the gigantic bulldozer.

The remainder of the Disney trip was wonderful, yet somewhat uneventful. Sadly, it was soon time to leave Florida and the families found themselves on a plane heading home. They had flown this route to Saskatoon multiple times and knew the flight plan would take them nearly over their own community. Ayden couldn't wait to look out of the window, from high above, and see a much smaller Quill Lake, that is, if the adventure had been real and not a dream.

As the plane flew across the flat prairies, both Ayden and his Dad were hoping to pick out the

Quill Lakes, a big enough landmark to be easily seen from the air. There the lakes were! And sure enough, Ayden could see how much less water was in and around them. Ayden's Dad noticed it too and was puzzled. By the time the family drove home from the airport it was dark, making it impossible to accurately judge the lakes' water levels. Ayden and his Dad would surly drive to the lake in the morning for a closer look, but tonight, the family would leave their suitcases packed and simply head to bed after a long day of travel.

Ayden opened his bedroom door, almost afraid to look inside. As he stepped onto his bedroom carpet, he immediately glanced at his shelves. All of the LEGO pieces he had built, remained sitting where he had left them; even the dust on the toys didn't appear to have been disturbed. Maybe, it had all been a weird dream after all. Ayden slipped on his pajamas and climbed high into his bunk. Soon his Mom and Dad came to tuck him in. As always, after his bedroom light was switched off, his night light automatically shone. Ayden noticed something shiny of his shelf, next to the excavator. The glow from his night light was making the diamond rock and gold nugget shimmer. Ayden smiled as he drifted off to sleep. The project and the journey had been real, after all.

In the morning, Ayden and his whole family drove out to Big Quill Lake. The surrounding area was much dryer than before. No one knew how the lengthy trench had been built but the area residents were as pleased as they were perplexed. More and more of the water-logged fields began to dry out as the excess lake water continued to flow northward.

One day, just as Ayden was about to head to the school bus, his Dad called out," Ayden, come here." Ayden ran to the truck, happy he wouldn't have to take the bus home.

"How come you're picking me up?"

"The girls have gone to dance class with Mom. I need your help with a project."

"What do I have to do?"

"Jump in bud, you'll see." Ayden and his Dad headed west and when they got close to the junction of highways 6 and 16, the truck pulled off to the side of the road. Father and son walked to the truck box where Ayden was handed tools and a post while his Dad lifted up a large, heavy, bronze plaque. What the two humans didn't know was that they had quite an audience that afternoon. Dozens of creatures were watching. Many of the work crew members sat camouflaged in the grass while Rickrack, Percy, Claw, Minnie and Casey crouched, hiding in the nearby shrubs. Slap and his entire family watched silently, just off shore, their brown heads barely above the water. Petunia, Piper and Poppy pelican swam nonchalantly in the pond, pretending to be out for a lazy, afternoon swim. Snowflake and Hayden sat nearby on matching telephone poles while Phil the eagle, soared high overhead doing dips and dives in celebration.

The two humans walked to a spot near the huge marsh. Ayden's Dad pounded the large post into the ground, upon which he carefully placed the bronze sign. Once it was securely in place, they both stood back and quietly read what the plaque explained. Ayden's Dad placed his arm around his son and gave a small nod. Grandpa Bruce's plaque was right back where it belonged!

Title: *Beads of Courage*®

(Oliver's Story)
- Author: Rosanna Gartley
- Publisher: MouseGate.com
- Paper Back: ISBN: 9781590952269
- eBook: ISBN: 9781590952320
- Number of pages in the finished book: 60
- Publication Date: April 25, 2017

Baby Oliver's life started out precariously in the neonatal intensive care unit. Each day, while he was a patient, his parents were given beads of various shapes and colors. Each bead symbolized a medical procedure that Oliver had endured on that day. By the time Oliver was discharged, his collection of beads was impressive.

As Oliver grew, his Beads of Courage® continued to hang on his bedroom wall. Not only were they a reminder of what he had lived through but also served as an inspiration for future challenges.

You won't want to miss what happens during a family vacation when this amazing little boy employs Disney magic to help those who need a little courage.

Title: *Castaway Crown*

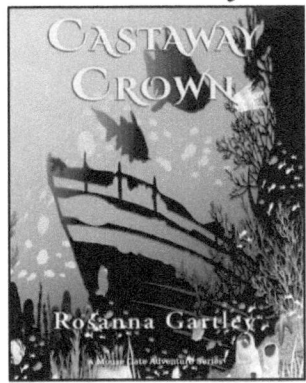

(Matthew and Anna's Undersea Adventure)
- Author: Rosanna Gartley
- Publisher: MouseGate.com
- Paper Back: ISBN: 9781590953327
- eBook: ISBN: 9781590953358
- Number of pages in the finished book: 60
- Publication Date: April 25, 2017

Matthew and Anna are full of excitement when they learn their family is going on a Disney cruise. With the magic of Disney both children are propelled into an adventure far below the ocean when they are asked to help the sea creatures get rid of a bothersome ghost. With Matthew's above average intellect coupled with Anna's amazing drawing abilities they solve the two-hundred-year old mystery bringing peace to the sea and the ghost.

Title: *Oh, Brother! Emily's Adventure*

- Author: Rosanna Gartley
- Publisher: MouseGate.com
- Paper Back: ISBN: 9781590953990
- eBook: ISBN: 9781590954003
- Number of pages in the finished book: 70
- Publication Date: April 25, 2017

    Emily, an only child adored by her parents, finds her life turned upside down and backwards when her parents welcome Adam, a foster child. During a family trip to Disney World, magic happens allowing Emily to alter the lives of those around her. Find out the agonizing decision Emily makes.

Title: *The Quill Lakes' Catastrophe*

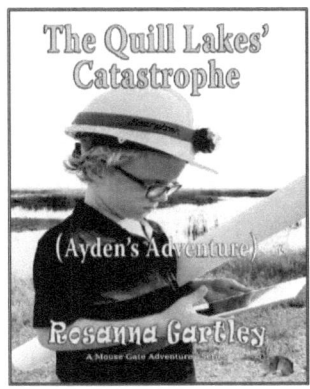

- Author: Rosanna Gartley
- Publisher: MouseGate.com
- Paper Back: ISBN: 9781590953549
- eBook: ISBN: 9781590953556
- Number of pages in the finished book: 96
- Publication Date: March, 06 2018

Eleven-year-old Ayden has lived on a farm near the Quill Lakes all his life. When the lakes' flooding puts his family at risk of losing their livelihood and way of life, something must be done. Ayden connects with some uniquely talented forest creatures, uses an ample dose of Disney Magic and relies on his own ingenuity to solve his community's water-logged problem.

The perfect Storytime book for both boys and girls ages 8–12 Grades: 3–6.

Author

Rosanna Gartley is the mother of four adult children, four bonus adult children and grandmother to 14. A retired nurse practitioner, she currently lives in southwestern Pennsylvania but hails from the Canadian prairies. Rosanna enjoys her family, most things creative and travelling with her husband, John.

Mouse Gate Adventure Series Books by Rosanna Gartley

This series of children's novels are the perfect story time reads for boys and girls ages 8-12. For the younger child, they make excellent 'read to' books that often deal with everyday situations faced by children in the real world.

Each novel's tale contains action and adventure spurred by an issue or dilemma. Fantasy is sprinkled into the mix with the help of Disney magic aiding the main character in solving the problem at hand. Rosanna's books not only entertain but educate as she weaves factual information throughout the entertaining chapters.

www.ingramcontent.com/pod-product-compliance
Lightning Source LLC
Chambersburg PA
CBHW030530080526
44586CB00011B/391